D0100110

SALT DOUGH

CREATIVE CRAFTS

SALT DOUGH

GREENWICH EDITIONS

Published in 1997 by Greenwich Editions
10 Blenheim Court, Brewery Road
London N7 9NT

Produced by Marshall Cavendish Books, London
(a division of Marshall Cavendish Partworks Ltd)

Copyright © Marshall Cavendish Ltd. 1997

All rights reserved. No part of this publication may be reproduced, stored in a retrieval
system or transmitted in any form or by any means electronic, mechanical, photocopying,
recording or otherwise, without the prior written permission of the publishers and the
copyright holder.

ISBN 0-86288-171-4

British Library Cataloguing in Publication Data:
A catalogue record for this book is available from the British Library

Printed and bound in France

Some of this material has previously appeared in the
Marshall Cavendish partwork *Get Crafty*

Marshall Cavendish Editorial Staff
Managing Editor: Ellen Dupont
Editor: Susie Dawson
Designer: Tim Brown
Production: Joanna Wilson

CONTENTS

Foreword

Like any other dough, salt dough is made of flour and water. Its difference lies in the addition of a huge proportion of salt to the basic ingredients, thus making it not only inedible but also long-lasting. The salt acts as a preservative. The technique of creating objects out of salt dough has been around since very ancient times. The ingredients are not expensive and are readily to hand in any kitchen. This means that the tradition of salt dough has always been a folk craft practised by the common people.

Once salt dough objects have been moulded they are baked for several hours in a slow oven to make them hard. For extra protection and durability they can be varnished after baking. Colour can be added either in the form of food colouring to the original dough or by painting the finished objects with poster or watercolour paints. Since baking the salt dough takes time, plan to make and bake the dough on one day and decorate it on another.

Salt dough can be used for making bowls and baskets, folk and fairytale figures, jewellery and seasonal decorations. The only limits to the possiblilities are your own patience and imagination. Since it requires little skill or expense to create an immediate effect, both children and adults alike can enjoy moulding their own creations.

You will need

FOR BASIC RECIPE:

100G / 4OZ PLAIN WHITE FLOUR

50G / 2OZ FINE TABLE SALT

10ML / 2TSP VEGETABLE OIL

60ML / 2½ FL OZ WATER

MIXING BOWL

ROLLING PIN

KNIFE

EGG AND WATER TO GLAZE

CLEAR VARNISH

working with salt dough

Use everyday household ingredients to make anything from bread baskets to seasonal decorations with a touch of traditional cheer.

Creating objects out of such basic ingredients as salt, flour and water is an ancient craft. Salt dough modelling has given generations of bakers an opportunity to show off their technical skills by adorning their shops with elaborate baskets, wreaths and festival loaves.

USE SALT DOUGH FOR • making seasonal decorations • bowls and baskets • folk and fairytale figures • novelty animals • jewellery.

For ceramic-hard results, salt dough is dried out very slowly by baking in an oven for about six hours at 145°C/290°F or three hours at gas 1½. Glazing prevents the dough from taking up moisture. When the bread has cooled completely, seal it with a coat of clear varnish.

MAKING COILS

1 Roll the dough into two long sausages of equal length using the palms of your hands. Cross over the two sausages in the middle and twist them tightly but gently together, working away from the centre. Do not pull the dough as it will stretch and break.

2 To join the ends of the coils, trim them with a knife. Separate the four ends, and cut each one diagonally so that they match when joined. To secure, wet the dough with a little water and press the ends together to complete the coil.

final touch

Bake the dough until hard, glaze with an egg yolk mixed with 15ml / 1tbsp water. Bake for 30 minutes. When cool seal with clear varnish.

MAKING LATTICE-WORK

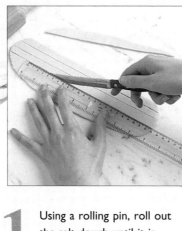

1 Using a rolling pin, roll out the salt dough until it is about 6mm / ¼in thick. Cut into strips 2cm / ¾in wide and place one strip across a wetted baking sheet. Lay the second strip over one end, at a right angle.

2 Keep laying more dough strips at right angles to each other, weaving them over and under the first and second strips. Continue in this way, lifting and replacing the strips as you add more until you have reached the end of the strips.

MAKING SALT DOUGH

1 Stir the flour and salt together in a large mixing bowl. Add the oil and water and mix thoroughly.

2 Knead the ingredients into a ball, adding a little more water, if necessary.

3 Turn the dough on to a flat, floured work surface. Continue to knead for about 10 minutes until the ball of dough is smooth and silky.

a lattice-work
BREAD BASKET

A lattice and coil salt-dough basket, glazed and varnished, will brighten up your breakfast table. Add some ears of wheat as a decorative touch and simply fill with oven-fresh rolls.

A pretty salt-dough basket filled with fragrant rolls is the perfect complement to a pot of freshly brewed coffee. Bread baskets have always been one of the traditional themes for salt dough, perhaps because the colours of bread and real wickerwork are so similar. They are also associated with the Harvest Festival, hence the salt-dough wheat-ear decoration.

Our basket is hard-wearing if treated with care. It has been designed for bread but you could fill it with fruit or vegetables and make it a feature of your kitchen decor.

You will need

1.1 LITRE / 2 PT PIE DISH

2 BAKING TRAYS

ALUMINIUM FOIL

SALT DOUGH

FOUR TIMES BASIC RECIPE, SEE PAGE 7

ROLLING PIN

KNIFE AND FORK OR SKEWER

SMALL PASTRY BRUSH

FOR GLAZING: 2 EGG YOLKS MIXED WITH 30ML / 2 TBSP WATER

CLEAR VARNISH

FAST-BONDING GLUE

making the basket

This pretty bread basket is easy to make and very decorative. It uses both the coiling and lattice salt-dough techniques.

1 Place the deep pie dish, base upwards, on a damp baking tray. Cover the dish with kitchen foil.

2 Roll out two lengths of salt dough, each about 25cm / 10in longer than the circumference of the dish itself. Put the remainder in a plastic bag to prevent it from drying out.

3 To make a coil, twist the two lengths of dough together (see page 8) and arrange it around the rim of the dish. Trim the ends neatly with a knife so that opposite ends butt up against each other. Moisten the ends and join them together (A).

4 Roll out the rest of the salt dough and cut it into thin strips about 1.2cm / ½in wide and long enough to go over the dish. Weave the lattice (see page 8) over the dish (B).

5 Wherever the dough crosses over dough, brush with a little water. To finish, trim the ends neatly with a knife. Brush the undersides with water and join them to the rim, piercing with a fork or skewer to secure the strips to the coil (C). Place another baking tray on top of the pastry-covered dish and press down firmly. This will ensure that the bread basket lies flat when in use.

A. Make a tight coil of salt dough around the rim of the upturned dish.

B. Weave the lattice by placing alternate strips of dough at right angles to each other.

C. Secure the strips to the coil by piercing them with a fork or skewer into the coil.

6 Place the basket in the oven and bake it for six hours at 145°C / 290°F or three hours at gas 1½. Tap the dough lightly at the end of the cooking time to check that it is hard. The dough should sound hollow if it is ready. If it sounds dull, bake it for a further 30 minutes. Glaze the outside with the egg mixture and bake for a further 30 minutes. Remove the basket carefully from the pie dish. Turn it the right way up and glaze the inside. Bake it for a further 30 minutes.

7 Turn the oven off, leaving the basket inside to cool. When the basket is completely cold, remove it from the oven and seal it with a couple of coats of clear varnish.

final touch

To decorate the basket with ears of wheat, roll small lumps of dough into almond shapes – you will need about 25. Snip diagonally up each shape. Bake the ears and allow them to cool. Attach the ears to the basket rim with fast-bonding glue, before painting with varnish to seal.

You will need

SALT DOUGH MADE WITH 3 CUPS FLOUR, 1 CUP SALT AND 1 CUP WATER

CARDBOARD TUBE

KNIFE AND SERRATED KNIFE

KITCHEN FOIL

ROLLING PIN

PAINTBRUSHES

ROSE LEAF, PRIMROSE, BLOSSOM AND CALYX CUTTERS

COCKTAIL STICKS

CLOVES

PLASTIC ICING NOZZLE WITH STAR-SHAPED END

GLASS-HEADED PIN

BAKING SHEET COVERED IN FOIL

SCISSORS

POSTER OR WATERCOLOUR PAINTS

POLYURETHANE VARNISH

napkin RINGS

Delicately decorated, these salt-dough napkin rings will add a touch of style to the dinner table. Painted in bright colours, they add an original finishing touch.

You may not use them every day, but these pretty napkin rings are perfect for those special occasions such as a dinner party or birthday party.

The flowers and leaves that decorate the rings are all made using cutters available from cake decorating shops. However, if you are good at modelling, you may be able to mould and shape the flowers straight from the dough.

The dough rings are so easy to make that you could let your guests take them home at the end of the evening as a souvenir, and bake some more for the next occasion. **USE NAPKIN RINGS FOR:** special birthdays • anniversary meals • Christmas dinner.

making the napkin rings

Make the dough following the instructions on page 8. Shape and bake the napkin rings a day or two in advance to allow yourself time for painting and varnishing them.

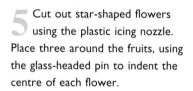

1 Make a support for the napkin rings: cut 5.5cm / 2¼in lengths from the cardboard roll with the knife. Cover each length with a piece of foil.

2 Roll out three sausages of dough about 25cm / 10in long and weave them into a tight plait. Turn the plait over and place a cardboard roll in the centre. Wrap each end of the plait around the roll and cut where the ends meet (A). Dampen each end with a paintbrush and join, pressing gently. Turn the roll upside down so the join is

B. Add some small flowers and leaves for decoration.

A. Plait the salt dough and wind the plait around the card.

underneath. Make sure the dough fits snugly around the roll.

3 To make the flowers, roll some dough out thinly and cut leaves with a cutter (B). Add veins with the back of a knife. Dampen the back of each leaf and then place five leaves on each napkin ring in a circle, with the points of the leaves facing outwards. Using the primrose and blossom cutters, cut some dough for each flower and place over the leaves, dampening the back of each

flower. Roll tiny balls of dough in the palm of your hand and place one in the centre of each flower. Pierce each primrose centre with a cocktail stick. Lightly mark the centres of the blossoms with a cocktail stick to add texture.

4 For oranges, roll out a sausage of dough and cut out three pieces of equal size. Roll into balls and mark with a cocktail stick to resemble orange skin. Push a clove into each orange, stalk end first. Dampen and arrange on the leaves.

C. Paint the rings with poster paints.

5 Cut out star-shaped flowers using the plastic icing nozzle. Place three around the fruits, using the glass-headed pin to indent the centre of each flower.

6 For the strawberries, make three small balls as for oranges but taper one end. Mark lightly with a cocktail stick. Cut out three calyx shapes and attach one to each strawberry end. Arrange on top of the leaves, adding four tiny dough blossoms. Place a ball of dough in the centre of each blossom.

7 Place the rings on a baking sheet covered with foil. Cover with foil and bake on the lower shelf of an oven at 100°C / 200°F / gas¼. Remove the foil after three hours and bake for a further three hours. Remove from the oven when rock hard and leave to cool.

8 Paint the napkin rings (C). Keep the colours bright and leave to dry. Apply two coats of clear polyurethane varnish, allowing the varnish to dry between coats.

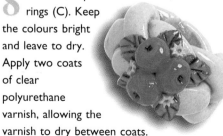

texturing salt dough

Specialist modelling tools are available to decorate salt dough, but you can use everyday household items and pastry and pasta cutters, as well as some cake decorating equipment.

Texturing salt dough allows you to add details to salt dough figures, leaves and flowers on wreaths and garlands as well as other novelty items. A wide variety of equipment can be used to texture salt dough, from everyday household implements such as a knife, fork, scissors and a cocktail stick, to specific cake decorating tools including crimpers and cutters, as well as a clay gun – originally used in clay work, as its name suggests, and now frequently used in cake decorating.

USE TEXTURED SALT DOUGH • to add interest and texture • to make wreaths and garlands • on figures.

You will need
SALT DOUGH
ROLLING PIN
RIBBED ROLLER
CRIMPING TOOL
PASTRY OR ICING CUTTERS
BRODERIE ANGLAISE CUTTERS
SCISSORS
CLAY GUN
KNIFE
FORK
COCKTAIL STICK

To make salt dough, see basic recipe on pages 7-8. As a general guide, the salt dough is baked at 145°C / 200°F / gas 1½, but this may vary, depending on the thickness of the salt dough item.

RIBBED TEXTURE

Roll out the dough in the usual way, using an ordinary rolling pin. Roll over the surface again using a ribbed roller and applying light pressure.

CRIMPING

Roll the salt dough out to the required thickness then use crimping tools, which are particularly useful for decorative edges, to achieve a variety of effects.

Crimper

Clay gun

CLAY GUN

Extrude the dough through a clay gun using a medium-sized simple fitment. The strands of dough are ideal for hair or for animal fur.

PLAITING

Rather than using a mass of extruded dough for hair, you can plait strands. Plaiting can also be used for baskets.

FORK

Use one or two household forks to texture more solid areas of dough to create a woven effect, as for a basket or hat.

SCISSORS

STAMPING

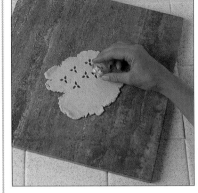

Use scissors to clip into the solid dough to create fur, hair or feather effects to use on animals or birds, for example on owls and hedgehogs, or to create a spiked effect. Scissors work best on balls of dough rather than rolled-out dough.

Broderie anglaise cutters are useful for stamping out small shapes to apply to other shapes, such as for ears and eyes on animals, or to create cut-out shapes as above.

Whoops

If the salt dough shapes aren't quite as you want them, simply knead the dough, roll it if necessary, and start again.

KNIFE

You can use a knife to produce less regular straight line texturing than a ribbed roller to use on three-dimensional rather than flat areas, for example to texture trousers or stockings as well as forming fingers on hands. A knife can also be used to cut strips of dough for bows.

COCKTAIL STICK

CUTTERS

A cocktail stick has a variety of possible uses, such as to create eyes, a nose and a mouth on a face, but it can also be used to create small regular holes in designs, for example to produce a lace effect on fabric. It can also be rolled on its side to create a fluted effect.

Roll out the salt dough and use cutters for simple shapes such as scallops and circles. You can also roll out the salt dough using a ribbed roller before cutting the shapes or combine cutters with crimping to make decorative shapes.

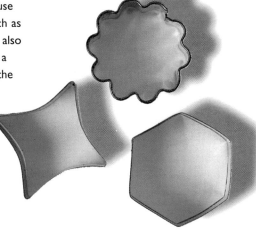

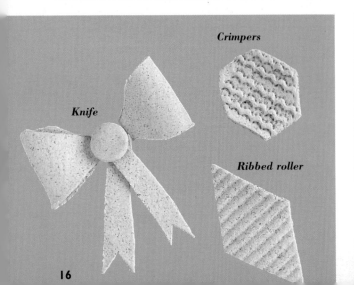

Scissors

Cocktail stick

Clay gun, plaited strands, and fork textures

final touch

Bake the salt dough until nearly dry then glaze it with an egg yolk mixed with 15ml / 1tbsp water. Bake for another 30 minutes. Leave to cool and then paint it if required. The finish can be sealed with a few coats of clear polyurethane varnish.

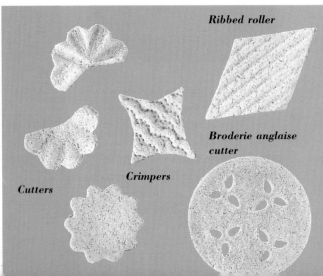

Crimpers

Knife

Ribbed roller

Ribbed roller

Broderie anglaise cutter

Cutters

Crimpers

salt dough
FIGURINE

Use salt dough to make this figure. The details and texturing are added with a variety of tools.

All sorts of novelty items, from toys to wall decorations, can be made out of salt dough. The figurine made here is 20cm / 8in tall although you can make it slightly larger if you like, but you'll have to increase the baking time slightly. Test the dough to see if it is ready by tapping it. It should sound hollow, as when baking bread. Don't be tempted to make it any smaller as it will become fiddly without much room for adding texturing and other details.

The figure is ideal for practising texturing salt dough using a variety of tools, most of which are readily available. Once baked, the figurine is completed by sealing it with a coat of clear polyurethane varnish. If you prefer, you can decorate it with artist's paints in the colours of your choice.

You will need

SALT DOUGH: TWICE THE BASIC RECIPE, SEE PAGE 7

COCKTAIL STICK

KNIFE

ROUND SCALLOPED CUTTERS

BRODERIE ANGLAISE CUTTERS

CRIMPERS

RIBBED ROLLING PIN

FORK

CLAY GUN

SCISSORS

BAKING TRAY

CLEAR OR TINTED, SATIN FINISH OR GLOSS POLYURETHANE VARNISH

PAINTBRUSH

making the figurine

To make the salt dough, use twice the quantity given in the basic recipe on page 7. Preheat the oven to 80°C / 170°F / gas low, to bake the dough. Assemble the figurine on a baking tray so you can place it directly into the oven without having to move it.

1 Make a thick triangle of dough for the body. Roll legs and mould the head. Add details to the face with a cocktail stick. Attach the head and legs using cocktail sticks in the joints (A) and smooth over the joints with water. Make sure the whole back is quite flat. Mark horizontal lines for the stockings on the legs.

A. Insert cocktail sticks into the body section and use them to secure the legs.

2 Make the petticoat using circular scalloped cutters on thinly rolled salt dough. Use a cocktail stick for the edging. Cut the circle in half and apply it in two layers using water. Mould the dough into shape if necessary.

3 Make the dress by rolling out the dough quite thinly and cut it to a rough skirt shape. Try it out over the figure and trim it to fit. Use broderie anglaise cutters to cut eyelets. Fit the skirt and crimp the edges with crimpers.

4 Roll out the dough using a ribbed roller and cut rough shapes for the bodice and apron of the pinafore. Use a double rib for the stripes on the pinafore. Cut a square of leftover ribbed dough for the pocket and texture it with a cocktail stick around the edge. Attach it to the body. Flatten balls of dough for buttons and make buttonholes with a cocktail stick.

5 Make the arms by rolling out sausages of salt dough and form into shape, fluting out the bases and hollowing them slightly ready to incorporate the hands. Attach to the shoulders using cut-down cocktail sticks. Roll out some dough, cut to shape for the sleeves and crimp the edges. Wrap the sleeves around the arms.

6 Mould a hat shape from a ball of dough and texture it with a fork to give a basket-weave effect. Make the hair by extruding the dough through a single hole in a clay gun and plait to form two braids, using a shorter piece for the fringe. Attach the hair to the head and then attach the hat.

7 To make the wheat, roll thin sausages of salt dough for the stalks and some for the ears, and use scissors to clip into the ears to texture them. Attach these to the front of the pinafore. Make the hands by rolling small balls of dough and flatten them. Use scissors to cut the fingers and attach the hands inside the sleeves.

8 Make the feet by rolling balls of dough and attaching them with water. To make bows, roll the dough very thinly, cut into strips and form bows. Attach these just above the ends of the plaits.

9 Bake for about two hours then turn the oven up to 100°C / 200°F / gas¼ for 30 minutes, then130°C / 250°F / gas½ for 30 minutes, then 150°C / 300°F / gas 2 until dry. Check by picking up the salt dough and tapping the base to see if it sounds hollow, as when baking bread.

10 Leave to cool overnight then varnish the figure, using clear or tinted varnish.

salt dough bowls

To make deep containers you need an ovenproof mould on which to bake the salt dough. A casserole dish or heat-proof mixing bowl is ideal.

You will need

SALT DOUGH
300G / 11OZ FLOUR
300G / 11OZ SALT
30ML / 2TBSP VEGETABLE OIL
200ML / 7FL OZ WATER
BASIC EQUIPMENT
CHOPPING BOARD
ROLLING PIN
MIXING BOWL
KNIFE
BAKING TRAY
SANDPAPER
VARNISH
PAINTBRUSH
BOWL FOR MOULD

You can use the bowls to hold bread or rolls or, alternatively, use them to display fruit or dried flowers. Fill the bowls with small chocolate eggs for Easter, or with pot pourri and place them in the hall to welcome your guests with perfume as they arrive. The possible uses for a salt dough bowl are only limited by your imagination.

The beauty of the salt dough is that you can add any texture, colour or finish that you wish. Food colourings can be used to colour the dough before it is baked, while poster paints, watercolours or acrylic paints can be used to further decorate a bowl that has first been coated with primer.

USE SALT DOUGH BOWLS • to hold pot pourri • to display fruit.

If you wish to give the dough a natural-looking shine, instead of painting it, apply a glaze of egg white, egg yolk or evaporated milk with a paintbrush before baking.

Craftytip

Bake the bowl as soon as it is finished. If you can't bake it immediately, cover the dough with clingfilm until you can.

1 Roll out the salt dough on a flour-dusted surface to approximately 12mm / ½in thick. Make sure it is wide enough to cover the bowl.

2 Wipe the outside of an ovenproof bowl with vegetable oil. Place the bowl upside down on the work surface. Place the dough over the bowl.

3 Smooth the dough down over the bowl with your hands, ensuring it sticks to the bowl. Cut away the excess dough around the rim of the bowl, then smooth the rim into place. Bake the bowl for 6 hours at a low temperature (about 100°C / 200°F / gas¼). When the dough has hardened, remove it from the oven.

4 Allow the dough to cool. Use some sandpaper to smooth over any rough edges on the bowl.

5 If you have not glazed the bowl, give it a protective coating by painting it all over with a few coats of varnish.

decorating BOWLS

Create a textured bowl, using salt dough and string, and decorate it to match your dinner service or table linen.

Interesting textures can be added to the surface of salt-dough bowls, using nothing more than a little ingenuity and basic tools.

Household string can be coiled and moulded to create simple patterns and shapes which are gently pressed into the surface of the salt-dough bowl. The bowl is baked and when the dough has hardened, the textured patterns are highlighted with some acrylic paint.

Other effects are created by making bowls from long coils of salt dough which are moulded round an ovenproof bowl or by colouring the salt dough before you begin moulding, using a few drops of liquid food colouring.

You will need

BASIC SALT DOUGH RECIPE SEE PAGES 7-8

ROLLING PIN

OVENPROOF BOWL

STRING

SHARP KNIFE

BAKING TRAY

SANDPAPER

VARNISH

PAINTBRUSH

PURPLE AND BLUE ACRYLIC PAINTS

GILT CREAM

making the bowls

To see if the dough has hardened, remove the bowl from the oven, and test its readiness by pressing on the thickest part of the bowl. If there is any give in the dough, bake it a little longer.

STRING SPIRAL BOWL

Interesting patterns can be created on the bowl by adding string.

A. Make a spiral shape on the salt dough using a length of string.

1 Roll the dough about 12mm / ½in thick and wipe the outside of your chosen bowl with vegetable oil. Place the bowl upside down on a work surface.

2 Place the dough over the bowl and smooth it down with your hands, so that it sticks to the bowl.

3 Cut lengths of string and press them to the side of the bowl in spirals (A).

4 Bake the bowl in the oven for about 6 hours at 100°C / 200°F / gas ¼. When the dough has hardened, remove it from the oven and allow to cool.

5 Apply a coat of purple acrylic paint. Leave the paint to dry and then apply a coat of varnish.

COILED BOWL

Roll coils of dough and use them to create a bowl.

1 Roll the salt dough into a long sausage. Wipe the outside of an oven-proof bowl with vegetable oil and place the bowl upside down on a clean work surface.

2 Carefully coil the sausage of salt dough around the bowl, making sure that you don't leave any large gaps between the coils (B). The coils will naturally bind together to form an unusually textured rope-like finish.

B. Coil the sausage of salt dough around an oven-proof bowl.

3 Bake the bowl as before and then leave to cool thoroughly. When the bowl is ready, paint with a coat of blue acrylic paint and then highlight areas with gilt cream.

COLOURED DOUGH

To colour the salt dough before moulding it to the oven-proof bowl, make a small well in the dough and pour in a few drops of liquid food colouring. Knead the dough well to disperse the colour evenly throughout. For brighter colours, try using paste food colourings.

building up
salt dough

Salt dough can be used to make individual pieces that are assembled during baking to build up into three-dimensional items, such as frames and letter racks.

S alt dough can be used to create three-dimensional as well as flat items. These are actually baked together in three-dimensional form, rather than baked flat, and then assembled afterwards with glue.

The pieces are cut and shaped in the required fashion, then baked for several hours in a slow oven. The pieces are allowed to cool, then they are joined together using more salt dough, smeared over the edges and moistened with a little water.

You can then stand the finished item supported on a baking tray,

and return it to the oven for several more hours, applying a little more salt dough glue during the baking. The salt dough glue binds the pieces together very firmly, making the finished item quite strong.

The finished piece can then be painted with ordinary emulsion paint or with artist's acrylic paint. Seal the salt dough with several coats of clear polyurethane varnish for an extra strong finish.

USE THREE-DIMENSIONAL SALT DOUGH • to make letter racks • for boxes • for picture frames.

You will need

ROLLING PIN AND RULER

BAKING PARCHMENT

SMALL POINTED KNIFE

DRINKING STRAW

OVEN-PROOF CONTAINER

FINE-GRADE SANDPAPER

ACRYLIC GESSO

ARTIST'S ACRYLIC OR EMULSION PAINT

PAINTBRUSHES

CLEAR SATIN POLYURETHANE VARNISH

FOR THE SALT DOUGH

4 CUPS PLAIN FLOUR

2 CUPS SALT

2 CUPS WATER

*M*ake the salt dough and roll it out 1cm / ³/₈in thick on baking parchment. Cut a rectangle 22x15cm / 8³/₄x6in for the back of the rack, a rectangle 22x8.5cm / 8³/₄x3¹/₂in for the front, and a strip 22x4cm / 8³/₄x1¹/₂in for the base.

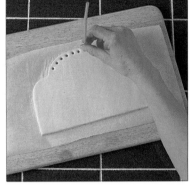

1 Cut away the corner on the upper long edge of the back and front to give a curved shape. Run a moistened finger along the cut edges to curve them gently.

2 Punch a row of holes on the upper edges of the back using a drinking straw. Bake the pieces in the oven at 120°C / 250°F / gas³/₄ for six and a half hours.

3 Allow the baked dough pieces to cool. Moisten the long cut edges of the base and smear with salt dough.

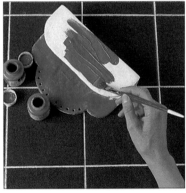

4 Moisten the lower, long edges of the back and front pieces. Press the back and front into position standing upright against the base. Support the back with an ovenproof container. Return the assembled piece to the oven for five hours until competely hard all over, smoothing more dough along the joins on the underside halfway through baking. Allow to cool.

5 Sand the salt dough, coat with acrylic gesso, leave to dry, then paint as required. Two shades of blue paint are blended here for the background. A sunflower in yellow and brown, and a couple of leaves in green are done free-hand. Apply five coats of varnish, leaving each coat to dry before applying the next.

salt dough PICTURE FRAME

Make and bake individual pieces of salt dough, assemble and join them with salt dough glue to make a frame with a nautical theme. Paint the frame and varnish it to finish.

You will need

PAPER, PENCIL AND SCISSORS, FOR TEMPLATE

FOR THE SALT DOUGH FOLLOW RECIPE ON PAGE 23

ROLLING PIN

BAKING PARCHMENT

SMALL, POINTED KNIFE

PIN

A FEW SHELLS

MASKING TAPE

FINE-GRADE SANDPAPER

WATERCOLOUR PAINTS

PAINTBRUSHES

CLEAR POLYURETHANE VARNISH

This complete picture frame, including the decorations, is made from salt dough. It is assembled stage by stage in the oven, and is baked for several hours after the addition of each new piece. You may need to plan your work over a couple of days to give yourself plenty of time to complete the various stages.

The stand needs to be well supported during the baking process – use scrunched up baking parchment on either side of it.

The finished frame is painted with watercolour paints. These will seep into the dough, giving an interesting texture and finish, but must be left to dry thoroughly before the frame is coated with clear polyurethane varnish.

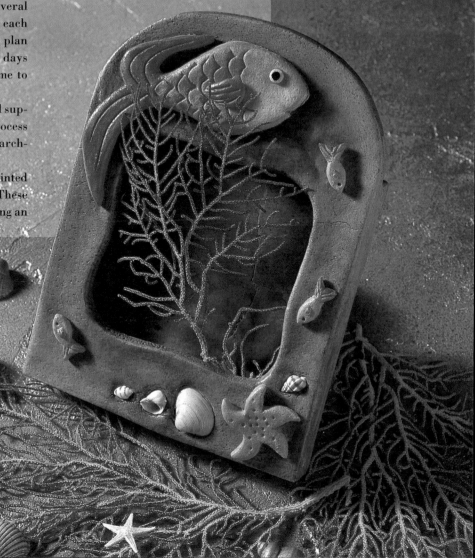

making the frame

Make the same quantity of salt dough as given in the recipe on page 23. The frame measures 15x20cm / 6x8in.

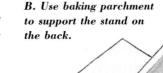

A. Moisten the salt dough and place the strips in position.

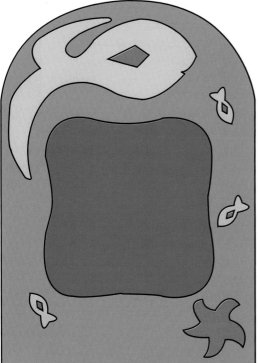

1 Enlarge the templates (above) to twice the size and cut them out. Roll some salt dough 6mm / ¼in thick on baking parchment. Cut out the large fish, three small fishes and a starfish, using the templates, and three 1cm / ⅜in wide strips. Set the strips aside. Pat the cut edges of the fishes and the starfish with a moistened finger to smoothe them.

2 Make a small diamond shape for the fins. Roll a small ball for the eye of the large fish. Moisten the fins and eye and press to the fishes. Indent the details on the fishes with the tip of a knife. Use a pinhead to dot the eyes of the small fishes and to decorate the starfish.

3 Roll the remaining dough 1cm / ⅜in thick on baking parchment. Cut out the stand and the front of the frame. Cut out the aperture. Run a moistened finger along the cut edges to curve them. Embed the shells into the frame front, leaving a space for the starfish. Cut a 15cm / 6in square of dough for the back.

4 Bake the fishes, starfish and frame front at 120°C / 250°F / gas ½, for 45 minutes, then allow to cool. Meanwhile, moisten the top of the frame back along three sides and place the strips on top, cutting the ends to fit the frame (A).

5 Moisten the underside of the partly baked fishes and starfish and smear with dough. Press in place on the frame front. Bake all the pieces in the oven for five hours as before. Leave to cool.

6 Moisten the top of the strips and smear with dough. Moisten the underside of the frame front along the straight edges. Press the front to the back, keeping the outer edges level. Return to the oven with the stand for two hours.

7 Moisten the shorter of the long stand edges and smear with dough. With the front face down and the slit opening at the top, moisten the back along the centre. Press the stand on top, then smear more dough along the join. Support the stand with scrunched up baking parchment at each side, secured in place with masking tape (B).

B. Use baking parchment to support the stand on the back.

8 Bake for two hours until completely hard, smoothing more dough along the front and back joins and around the stand after one hour. Allow to cool. Lightly sand the frame.

9 Paint the frame and leave to dry for at least six hours. Apply five coats of varnish, allowing each coat to dry before applying the next. Use a small paintbrush to apply varnish into the corners.

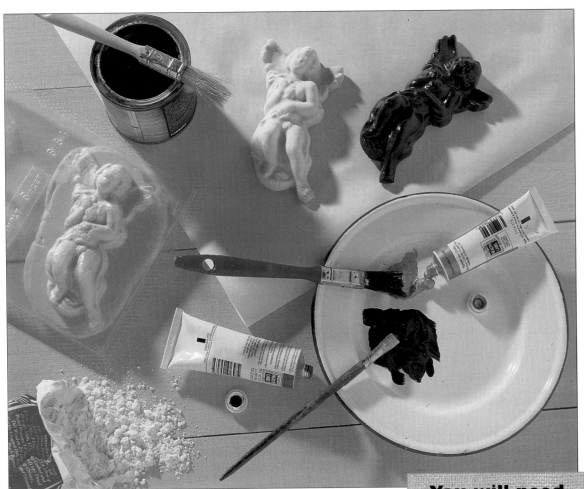

distressing salt dough

The salt dough is shaped in a mould, baked and then given a distressed finish. The final effect is like that of burnished, gilded plaster.

You will need

SALT DOUGH (HALF THE QUANTITY GIVEN IN BASIC RECIPE ON PAGE 7)

CORNFLOUR

CHERUB CAKE DECORATOR'S MOULD

SHARP KNIFE OR SCALPEL

BAKING TRAY

BROWN ACRYLIC PAINT

GOLD OIL PAINT

CLEAR GLOSS POLYURETHANE VARNISH

BRUSHES

The distressed, burnished paint effect is achieved by painting the salt dough with brown acrylic paint, then gloss, then gold oil paint, brushed on with a dry brush to catch the raised surfaces only. You can use a variety of colours as a base coat to good effect as long as they are reasonably dark. Try deep, dark red, dark green and terracotta, all of which are suitable for highlighting with gold paint. A coat of varnish applied to the finished effect, back and front, protects the finish to make it long lasting.

The cherubs created here make a wonderful decoration to use as a wall plaque or a free-standing decoration on a dresser or mantelpiece. Make a collection of these novelty salt dough items for a festive decoration or to give as gifts. The finished effect is that of painted plaster models.

USE DISTRESSED SALT DOUGH • to make seasonal decorations • for novelty items • for wall plaques.

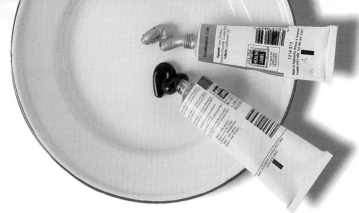

Make the salt dough and preheat the oven to 100°C / 200°F / gas low. Dust the mould lightly with cornflour to prevent the salt dough from sticking to it. A coat of brown paint is used as a base for the gold but you can also use other colours – dark blue, turquoise, dark green and a deep red are all suitable.

1 Work the salt dough well into the mould, ensuring that it fills all the crevices of the design. Use your fingers to press it in well, working from the centre outwards to avoid air bubbles.

2 Turn the dough out and trim away the excess dough with a knife. Set on a baking tray, bake for I hour, increase temperature to 130°C / 250°F / gas ½ and bake for 2 hours.

3 Allow the dough to cool, then paint with brown acrylic paint, working it well into all areas of the surface.

final touch

Once the gold paint is dry, apply a coat of clear gloss varnish to seal and protect the finish.

4 Paint the dough with a coat of clear gloss varnish, working into all the indents on the surface and being careful not to allow any drips to form. Leave to dry.

5 Brush gold paint lightly over the surface of the salt dough, keeping the brush as dry as possible so that only the raised areas are highlighted. Leave until completely dry.

You will need

2 CUPS PLAIN FLOUR

1 CUP SALT

1 CUP WATER

BLUE AND RED FOOD COLOURING

GLASS CABOUCHON JEWELLERY STONES

ROLLING PIN

BAKING PARCHMENT

BAKING SHEET

SMALL KNIFE

DRINKING STRAW

DRESSMAKING PIN

GOLD METALLIC POWDER, FROM CAKE DECORATING SUPPLIERS

SOFT ARTIST'S PAINTBRUSH

CLEAR SATIN FINISH POLYURETHANE VARNISH

PAINTBRUSH

LEATHER OR COTTON THONGING

TWO PENDANT HOLDERS

TWO EARRING WIRES

salt dough JEWELLERY

Make this chunky jewellery out of salt dough, coloured with food colouring and studded with sparkling cabouchons.

You can colour the salt dough before you bake it, using food colouring rather than painting the baked items. Colouring it this way produces a lovely soft colour, which you can enhance by brushing with a little gold metallic powder before you bake the pieces. Be careful when adding the food colouring to the salt dough – add one or two drops at a time and knead it in to check the colour before adding more. The colour is quite strong and if you add too much, it will also make the dough too wet.

You don't need to glue the stones to the jewellery – it is quite safe to bake the pieces with them in place as the heat is so low. Use a pinhead to indent a design around the edges of each piece.

Apply several coats of varnish to the finished pieces to protect the finish. Salt dough jewellery is surprisingly strong and provided you don't knock it sharply it is unlikely to shatter.

making the jewellery

For details of making salt dough, follow the instructions given on page 8.

B. Use a pinhead to indent the outside edge of the dough.

1 Make the salt dough and divide it into thirds. Gradually knead in the food colouring to make one third red and the other two thirds blue. Add a little more flour if the dough becomes too wet.

2 Form the red dough into a ball. Roll out to about 8mm / ⁵⁄₁₆in thick then cut the heart shape using the template.

3 Punch a hole for hanging at the top of the heart with the drinking straw (A).

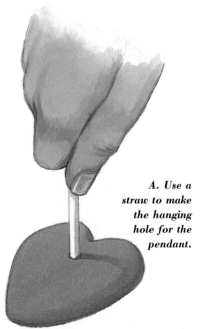

A. Use a straw to make the hanging hole for the pendant.

4 Roll the blue salt dough out flat, 6mm / ¼in thick on baking parchment. Use the template to cut two stars.

5 Using a pin, pierce holes at the top of the stars for hanging. Turn the pin to make the holes 3mm / ¹⁄₈in wide.

6 Arrange the cabouchon stones on the heart and stars and then press them into the dough. Indent a row of dots around the edges with a pinhead (B). Use a soft brush to brush gold metallic powder lightly over the surfaces.

7 Place the pieces on a baking sheet and bake at 120°C / 250°F / gas ½ for five hours until hard. Leave to cool in the oven.

8 Apply five coats of varnish, remembering to varnish inside the hanging holes as well. Leave until completely dry.

9 Knot the heart pendant on to a length of thonging. Fix a pendant holder to the stars then attach to the earring wires.

Templates for the star and heart

salt dough
WALL
PLAQUE

This salt dough wall plaque adds a colourful touch to the kitchen or a child's room. Do not be afraid to use your own design skills to make up a plaque to suit a particular room or occasion.

Hansel and Gretel would feel at home in this quaint little cottage, especially as there's no witch in sight. The bad news is that it's not made of sugar, so they can't eat it. The colours used here are traditional but you can use any colours you like. If you don't have poster or watercolour paints, knead food colouring into the dough instead to add colour. The final effect will be paler and more pastel-like than when using paint.

Some of the shapes are cut with pastry and aspic cutters. If you don't have these, use the cutters you have or, for example, change the tiles from heart shapes to the more traditional tile shape and overlap them when making the roof.

You will need
350G / 12OZ PLAIN FLOUR
100G / 4OZ SALT
225ML / 8FL OZ WATER
THIN CARD
ROLLING PIN
KNIFE
PLUNGER CUTTER FOR FLOWERS
ASPIC CUTTER FOR LEAVES
HEART-SHAPED PASTRY CUTTER
KITCHEN FOIL
BAKING SHEET
POSTER PAINTS
PAINTBRUSHES
RIBBON
GOLD THREAD
5CM / 2IN PIECE OF
WIRE OR HAIRPIN
CLEAR GLOSS
POLYURETHANE
VARNISH OR YACHT VARNISH

making the plaque

Baking the salt dough takes time, so make and bake the dough on one day and decorate it later. If you don't have the necessary cutters, cut the shapes with a sharp, pointed knife – although it will take longer than using the cutters.

1 Make the dough as described in the method on page 8. Make a template of the house on card using the outline given on this page. Cover the baking sheet with kitchen foil. Roll the dough out on a lightly floured surface to a thickness of 6mm / ¼in. Place the template on the dough and cut out the house shape (A).

A. Cut out the house shape.

C. Push a wire loop through the top.

2 Lift the dough on to the baking sheet. Create a brick pattern on the chimney by indenting the dough with the back of a knife. Roll out more dough until it is 3mm / ⅛in thick. Cut out ten heart shapes. Moisten the back of each one using a paintbrush and place them on the roof. Cut out a door, place on house and indent it with the back of the knife to resemble slats of wood (B). Roll a tiny ball of dough for the doorknob, cut out two small sets of hinges and make window frames. Moisten and add to the house. Cut out leaves and flowers and arrange around the windows.

3 Push a wire loop into the top (C). Bake at 100°C / 200°F / gas ¼ on the lower shelf of the oven. After five hours, peel the foil off, turn the dough over and place in the oven again until completely dry all the way through. It should sound hollow when tapped. Turn the oven off and allow the dough to cool completely in the oven.

4 Decorate the cottage with poster paints (D). Leave to dry and apply three coats of varnish, allowing it to dry between coats.

B. Indent the dough.

final touch

Remove the wire loop at the top. Pull the gold thread through the hole by looping it with a piece of wire. Add a length of ribbon and tie a neat bow.

D. Paint the dough.